The Public Sector

Living and working in moder

Written by Christopher Yeates

Illustrated by Zoe Sadler

Note to teachers:

The content of this book expands and elaborates on the themes presented in the Key Stage 2 series by the same author. In some places the text and accompanying illustrations from the Key Stage 2 books are reproduced here verbatim, or in very similar form.

© Gresham Books 2017
Published by Gresham Books Limited
The Carriage House, Ningwood Manor, Ningwood,
Isle of Wight PO30 4NJ
ISBN 978-0-946095-90-2

Printed in Great Britain

CONTENTS

Introduction   4

Introducing the public sector   6

Calling the emergency services   8

The emergency services   10

Refuse collectors   14

Looking after Britain's roads   16

Providing an education for every child   18

Treating Britain – the NHS   20

The national safety blanket – social care services   23

Keeping Britain safe – the armed forces   25

The Prime Minister and the Cabinet   27

Managing Britain's money – the budget   30

Do you remember?   32

BRITISH VALUES

Britain is made up of England, Wales and Scotland, and the people who live in these countries are called British. The people of Northern Ireland may also call themselves British and together we make up the United Kingdom. This book is to help you learn about and come to understand some of the British Values we all share.

INTRODUCTION

Critical thinking – how to read this book

In this book you will be asked to debate and evaluate situations and then decide what you think. When you debate, evaluate and decide, you are using your powers of critical thinking.

Learning to become a strong critical thinker will help you think clearly and rationally about what to believe, say, write and do.

The processes of critical thinking provide you with a series of steps to help you analyse, evaluate, debate and decide what you think about situations or choices for yourself.

Step 1: Analyse

What are the facts of the situation or choice?
How do you know the facts are true? Is there any evidence? Is the evidence trustworthy?

Step 2: Debate

Consider all points of view – especially if you disagree – and let everyone have their say. Do you have reasons to support your views? Is there evidence to support your point of view or that of others? Do you think this evidence is strong or weak?

Step 3: Keep an open mind

Are you being open-minded? Are you prepared to listen to the reasons of others and change your mind if their reasons are persuasive? Being prepared to be open-minded is an essential part of becoming a strong critical thinker.

Be honest with yourself. Check for prejudice. Are you being prejudiced? Are others being prejudiced?

Step 4: Evaluate

What are the strengths and weaknesses of the arguments behind each point of view? How strong is the evidence supporting these arguments?

Step 5: Decide

Reflecting on every point of view, and the reasons and evidence you have heard, decide what you think.

To double-check whether you have genuinely been open-minded, ask yourself:

- What is the strongest reason supporting your decision?

- What single piece of evidence helped you decide?

- What reason or piece of evidence might change your mind?

What we mean when we say...

Evaluate: identify the strengths and weaknesses.
Analyse: examine something in detail.
Evidence: facts provided to help prove something is true or false.
Prejudice: a preconceived opinion that is not based on facts or personal experience.

CHAPTER 1: INTRODUCING THE PUBLIC SECTOR

A country is nothing without the people who live in it. The public sector provides a series of services that help look after Britain. Looking after Britain really means looking after the **people** of Britain, and keeping them happy. People just like you. It makes sense that people who are *organised*, *provided* for, *cared* for, and kept *safe* have a very good chance of being **happy**.

But perhaps you think you don't need looking after. Well, maybe you're right. But have a think about this. Every day, there are an awful lot of things which we just assume will simply *happen*, without us even having to think about it. Your life would be very different without these things – and not in a good way.

For a start, you wouldn't be at school. Okay, some of you might think that wouldn't be so bad. But how would you feel if when you got sick, there were no doctors or nurses to look after you? What if your house was on fire, and fire engines didn't exist? What if nobody ever built any roads, or collected your rubbish?

It's not a pretty picture, is it? Without a system to look after Britain and its citizens, the country would be in a bit of a mess. Luckily, there is such a system. This system is called the *public sector*. The public sector is probably the most important thing in your life you've never heard of.

Looking after a whole country is an absolutely massive job. This is why the responsibility of looking after Britain is **shared** between lots of different groups of people. All of these groups are part of the public sector. These groups all look after a different part of Britain, but are all doing the same job: looking after the well-being of our country. These groups are organised by the *Government* of the country. The point of these groups is to provide *services*, which everybody in the UK can use. These services include schools, hospitals, roads, the police, the military – and many other useful things besides.

6

Think about your body. Each bit of you is extremely good at one particular job. Each bit of your body has a special job, and relies on the other bits of the body to do their special jobs. If all the bits do their job properly, we have a happy person – you.

The public sector is a lot like your body. It is a single thing, but it is made up of lots of **different parts**. Each of these parts has a special job in looking after Britain, just like the different parts of your body have a special job in looking after you. When all of these parts are working well together, better services are provided to the people of Britain. Some of these parts will be quite familiar to you. Other parts won't be quite so obvious, but are just as important.

What we mean when we say...

Government: the group of people that we have chosen to lead our country.

Public Sector: services provided by the Government that help look after the needs of the people. Britain's public sector includes services like providing schools, hospitals and the police.

Debate and evaluate:

In a group, discuss:

1 What kind of public sector services have you used this week? For example, these might include your school, seeing a doctor, using roads or motorways. Which of these are most important to you?

2 What kind of services do you think a Government should provide for its people?

3 Carry out a survey in your group. Which public services do you think are the most important? Explain why.

Read, research and decide:

1 Explain in your own words what we mean by the public sector.

2 Write a paragraph explaining why you think it is important for a Government to provide public services for its people.

3 Write an account of a public service that people depend on. What do you think would happen without this public service?

CHAPTER 2: CALLING THE EMERGENCY SERVICES

It is highly likely that at least once in your life, you will ring **999**. Perhaps this is something you have done already. 999 is the number we phone when we see, or are involved in, a scary, dangerous situation that we cannot deal with on our own. Luckily, we do not have to deal with it on our own. Instead, Britain has its very own team of superheroes, and to summon them to your side, all you have to do is dial three numbers: 999. These superheroes are the men and women in our country's *emergency services*. They are highly trained experts who know how to tackle even the scariest, most dangerous situation.

The emergency services have two main jobs:
* In a 999 emergency, to provide *care* and rescue.
* To keep us *safe* by preventing 999 situations from happening in the first place.

999 is the number you dial if you need help in an emergency. When you dial this number, you can ask for the help of:
* Police
* Ambulance Service
* Fire Brigade
* Coastguard

When you dial 999 an *operator* will ask you:
* What service you require.
* Your name and where you are calling from.

You will then be put through to the emergency service you have requested. When you have been put through to the emergency service you can tell them what is wrong and the address of the problem.

But it is very important that you only ever dial 999 in a real emergency. Never make a false call. This could risk the lives of others who really need the help of an emergency service and you will be breaking the law.

Everyone in Britain owes a great deal to the men and women in the police, fire, ambulance and coastguard services. Every day, they risk their lives to keep all of us as safe and cared for as possible.

What we mean when we say...

Emergency Services: public services (police, ambulance, fire brigade, coastguard) that help people in an emergency.

Debate and evaluate:

In a group, discuss:

1 Make a list of emergency situations that you think the emergency services could be called to.

2 Role play in a group taking on the roles of emergency telephone operator and someone calling for help. Imagine that you are calling for emergency help in the following situations:
   - You see a house on fire.
   - You see a car accident and the driver seems to be badly injured.
   - You are on the beach and see some swimmers in the sea who seem to be in trouble and need help.

Read, research and decide:

1 Describe in your own words what you should do in an emergency. What number should you call and what information should you provide?

2 Explain why you should only ever dial 999 in a real emergency.

3 Why do you think it is important to stay calm in an emergency?

CHAPTER 3: THE EMERGENCY SERVICES

The Police

There are a number of situations where the police will be called into action. These include:
- If there has been a serious road **accident**.
- If somebody is seriously **injured**.
- If somebody is feeling **threatened** by another person.
- If a **crime** has been committed, or is about to be committed.

To react as quickly as possible to an emergency situation, police cars have loud sirens and flashing blue lights to let other drivers know they should make way for them on the road.

Once the police arrive, the first thing they do is make the scene **safe**, so that no more people become involved in the emergency. They then deal with the situation. This might mean making an *arrest*, or giving *first aid* to somebody who has been injured in a car crash. They might also collect *evidence* from the scene, which could be used to prove to a court what happened. But the work of the police does not stop at the scene. If the police suspect a crime has been committed, they will search for *suspects* on the run, and for victims who may have gone missing.

Keeping us safe by stopping dangerous situations from happening in the first place is just as important as being on hand to save the day when things do go wrong. That is why you will see police on patrol, looking out for suspicious behaviour and making people think twice before causing any trouble. If you ever feel like something is wrong in your neighbourhood, or you want to talk about something that's worrying you, seek out your friendly local Police Community Support Officer (PCSO).

The Fire Brigade

Fires are extremely dangerous. Even small fires can very quickly become big, scary fires. This is why it is always important to ring 999 as soon as you can so that you give the fire service plenty of time to react to your emergency. Like police cars, fire trucks have loud sirens and flashing lights to help them get to your side as quickly as possible. A fire truck is a very special truck indeed, and is every firefighter's best friend. Each truck has multiple water hoses, which means several firefighters can shower the fire at once. Every truck carries enough hose to stretch the length of three football fields. They also carry several ladders, which firefighters can use to rescue people trapped at the top of burning buildings.

While the main job of the fire service is to keep Britain safe by putting out fires, they also have another, very important job: stopping fires from starting in the first place. This is why members of the fire brigade spend a lot of time going to schools, offices and people's houses to give advice on fire safety. They also inspect the buildings they visit to check that if a fire does break out, it has useful equipment like *fire extinguishers*. Finally, firefighters make sure everyone in the building knows the *evacuation drill*. You have probably practised these drills before. If the school fire alarm went off right now, would you know where to go?

The Ambulance Service

The main job of the ambulance service is to provide emergency medical treatment and care to people who have been injured in a dangerous situation, or who have suddenly become very ill. There are two parts to the emergency side of their job:

- To get the injured or sick person to hospital as quickly as possible.
- To help the injured or sick person as much as they possibly can on the way to the hospital. This is usually the job of *paramedics*, who are specially trained in emergency first aid.

The ambulance service is often called to support the police and fire emergency officers, because dangerous situations mean it is very likely that people will need medical help. As you can imagine, in medical emergencies, every second counts. This is why the ambulance service sometimes use helicopters to get to remote places, such as at the top of mountains or in the middle of the countryside.

So, do you feel safer, knowing that help for every type of scary situation is only a 999 call away? It's pretty incredible to think that just because you live in Britain, experts are on call 24/7 to help you out of any sticky situation. Everyone in Britain owes an awful lot to the men and women in the police, fire and ambulance services.

What we mean when we say...

Emergency Services: public services that help people in an emergency (police, ambulance, fire brigade, coastguard).

Evidence: facts or information that help us work out if something is true.

Suspect: the person accused of committing a crime.

Paramedic: a person trained to carry out emergency first aid but who is not a doctor.

Debate and evaluate:

In a group, discuss:

1 What kind of personal skills and qualities do you think you need to become a member of the emergency services?

2 Make a list of emergency situations that you think the police could be called to.

Read, research and decide:

1 If you were to join one of the emergency services which one would you join? Explain why.

2 Write an account explaining in what ways you think members of the emergency services help look after and protect us. Try to include examples to support your ideas.

CHAPTER 4: REFUSE COLLECTORS

Some members of the public sector are harder to spot than the sirens and flashing lights of the emergency services. These include the people who collect our rubbish, who maintain our roads, and who help look after public spaces.

Have you ever wondered how it is you have mountains of rubbish one minute, and the next an empty bin, ready to be re-filled? Refuse collectors – or binmen – help to look after Britain by getting rid of our waste in a safe, organised way.

Binmen are early risers and are often beginning their working day before 6am. Their lorry is no ordinary lorry; it's called an RCV, or a *Refuse Collection Vehicle*. Using a powerful lifting mechanism, RCVs can easily empty heavy bins into the huge container at the back of the lorry. Once inside the RCV, the rubbish is cut up by a giant blade, and squished down so that there is room for the binmen to collect as much waste as possible. There are three different types of waste that they collect: waste from people's houses, waste from people's gardens, and waste which can be *recycled* (broken down and used again). A number of different substances can be recycled, for example, glass, paper and metals.

Many binmen collect rubbish from 1600 houses in a single day, and walk over 15 miles. Sometimes, they do all this in the pouring rain, which is why they are given special clothing to wear. This clothing has trousers with *fluorescent* markings, so that even in bad weather, people can see them.

At the end of the day, the lorry returns to the depot where the RCVs are stored. At the depot, all the waste that has been collected that day is sorted into enormous, separate piles.

What we mean when we say...

Refuse: another word for rubbish.

RCV: Refuse Collection Vehicle. The special lorry used to collect and deal with your rubbish.

Recycle: use again. A lot of our rubbish can be recycled and converted into useful items.

Debate and evaluate:

In a group, discuss:

1 Why do you think it is necessary for our Government to provide a system of refuse collection? What problems might there be if our rubbish was not collected?

2 Why is recycling important? What actions can you take to encourage more people to recycle items?

Read, research and decide:

1 Research and write an account of what happens to a piece of rubbish from your home.

2 Carry out your own research on what kind of materials can be recycled. Do you think your family could do more recycling at home? Remember to give examples to support your ideas.

CHAPTER 5: LOOKING AFTER BRITAIN'S ROADS

Most of us use roads every single day. Think about how you get to school every morning, or how you go to see your friends, or go on holiday. Unless you can take the train or fly, you probably use several different roads, roads which allow us to travel all over the country.

Motorways, roads and lanes are all maintained for us by the public sector. Road workers play a key role in looking after Britain by providing the *infrastructure* (or framework) for cars, buses, lorries and bikes.

Road workers *care* for the roads they build by fixing things like potholes in our roads. Many drivers get frustrated at having to sit in traffic because road workers are improving or mending the road. But it is important to remember that everything would grind to a halt if these **essential repairs** were not carried out.

Road workers also put up all the **signs** you see on the road which tell people how to get to the places they want to go, and paint the white marks you see which tell people which side of the road to drive on.

A lot more people than you might imagine are involved in helping to keep Britain's roads safe and usable. In the winter months you will probably have seen big gritting lorries driving on roads near where you live. Their job is to scatter salt when ice and snow are expected, so that ice doesn't form and make roads slippery and dangerous. In the summer months you might see people cutting back plants and hedges, which can sometimes become overgrown, especially on smaller roads.

Britain has an astonishing 245,000 miles of road, which is enough to wrap around the world ten times. Ten! That's a lot of road to look after...

What we mean when we say...

Infrastructure: a framework. Roads are an important part of a country's infrastructure.

Debate and evaluate:

In a group, discuss:

1 Make a list of items that you use that will have been transported by road. Are any of these items essential for living?

2 Why do you think our country needs motorways?

Read, research and decide:

1 What reasons do your family have for the journeys they make by road? For example, to go to work, school, visit friends or family, to pursue hobbies or other pleasure interests.

2 How many roads do you use each week? How would your life change if these roads did not exist?

CHAPTER 6: PROVIDING AN EDUCATION FOR EVERY CHILD

The public sector looks after Britain by providing teachers and schools, so that every single child in the country can go to school and be educated until they are at least 16 years old. Providing an *education* for every child and young person is a very important part of the work of the public sector.

Why do you think it is so important to be educated? Of course, there are hundreds of reasons why being educated makes a positive difference to people and the countries they live in.

- Going to school teaches you about the **world** you live in, and how you can make a positive difference to the world around you.
- Going to school lets you take control of your **future**. Being educated will mean you know how to look after yourself. School will provide you with the skills you need to earn a living doing a job you enjoy, and make a valuable contribution to our society.
- Going to school doesn't just teach you about facts. At school, you learn how to make **friends**, how to **behave** around people, how to become **confident**, and what **right and wrong** mean to you.
- The harder you try at school and the more educated you become, the more these good things will become a positive part of your life. It might not seem like it right now, but going to school to be educated is one of the most important things you will ever do.

Obviously, the public sector needs to provide schools for us all to go to. But it is not really the schools themselves that are important. It is the *people* inside the schools, who are there every single day you are (and sometimes on other days too), working to make sure your education is the best it can possibly be: people like your **teachers**, who all through your school life are there to help you learn about the world; teaching assistants who also help support your learning; people like **librarians**, who make sure you have books to read; people like **cooks** who make the food to help power your brain, and the **sports coaches** who train your body, and the **IT wizards** who you have to thank for the computers you get to use. All of these people will be a big part of your life until you are at least 16. However, lots of people stay in school until they are 18, and then go on to university – where you might even learn how to become a doctor or a nurse, a road engineer, or a teacher yourself!

Debate and evaluate:

In a group, discuss:

1 What are the most important things you have learnt at school so far?

2 Why do you think it is important that every child has the opportunity to go to school?

Read, research and decide:

1 Write a paragraph explaining why you think every child should have the chance to go to school.

2 What are the benefits to our country of having well educated citizens? Remember to include examples to support your ideas.

CHAPTER 7: TREATING BRITAIN – THE NHS

The National Health Service, or NHS, is one more very important way that the public sector provides for us, cares for us and helps keep us safe.

The NHS was set up in 1948, just after World War Two. After the terrible destruction and suffering of the war, the Government felt that a service should be created that would treat anyone who was ill, whether they were rich or poor, young or old. For your whole life, if you have a medical problem, no matter how severe, you will be looked after.

Which part of the NHS you use depends on how badly ill or hurt you are.

Your local GP

A GP is your local doctor. GP is short for general practitioner. **General practitioners** (GPs) treat patients with a variety of common medical conditions and refer – or send on – patients to hospitals and other medical services for urgent and specialist treatment. GPs focus on the health of the whole person combining physical, psychological and social aspects of care. GPs work side by side with *nurses*, who work in many different areas of the NHS.

Specialists

If a medical problem is more complicated, the GP might send you to see a specialist in a hospital. This is called a *referral*. GPs know something about all the parts of your body. Specialists know a great deal about one specific part of your body, like your heart or your throat.

Off to A&E

If you have an accident, you are likely to be taken to the Accident & Emergency department – often known as A&E.

Most hospitals have an A&E service. When you get there, somebody, usually a nurse, will assess how urgently you need to be treated. This is called *triage*. This is a process where everyone who arrives at A&E is assessed to decide who has the most urgent medical needs.

For example, if you went to A&E because you had fallen off your bike and hurt your arm, even though your wounded arm might be painful, it makes sense that the poor man you can see in the picture, who has suddenly arrived in an ambulance because he can't breathe and might die, is treated before you are.

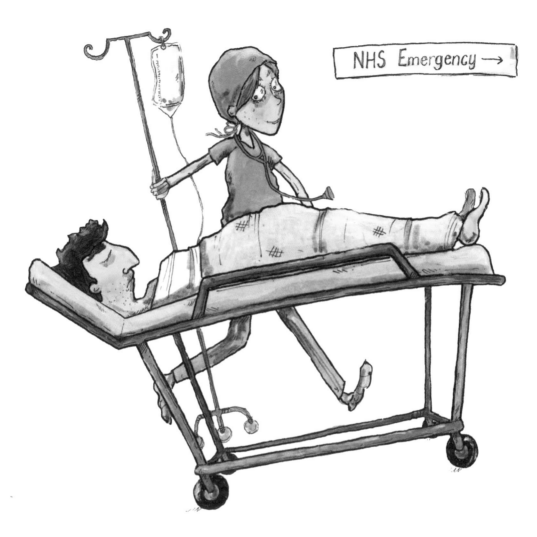

NHS Emergency →

Despite the fact that the NHS is very expensive to run, many countries envy Britain's system of providing free medical care for all.

The NHS Army

There are many different types of medical care, and the type you receive will depend on what is wrong with you. But as well as all the doctors, nurses and paramedics, there is a whole army of people who work for the NHS who are not on the frontline of making people better, but are still incredibly important. Cleaners, cooks, receptionists, porters, ambulance drivers, nursing assistants – there is always so much going on if you look closely enough, and the NHS simply wouldn't be able to look after you without the support of these members of staff.

What we mean when we say...

National Health Service (NHS): the organisation that provides free health care to Britons.

General Practitioner or GP: a doctor who treats a wide variety of medical problems, but is not a specialist.

Specialist: a doctor who has had extra training to become an expert in a particular aspect of medicine.

Referral: the directing of a patient to see a medical specialist.

Triage: the assignment of degrees of urgency to wounds or illnesses to decide the order of treatment of a large number of patients or casualties.

Debate and evaluate:

In a group, discuss:

1 The NHS provides free health care for all Britons. Why do you think it is so important to provide all citizens with access to free medical care?

2 What do you think are the benefits of the triage system?

Read, research and decide:

1 Your local GP surgery provides a wide range of care. Carry out your own research on the different types of health services provided by your local GP surgery.

2 Thousands of people are employed by the National Health Service. Carry out your own research and write an account of the different types of careers you could pursue in the National Health Service.

CHAPTER 8: THE NATIONAL SAFETY BLANKET – SOCIAL CARE SERVICES

Social care services are another form of care provided for Britons by the Government. **Social care** in England is defined as the provision of **social** work, personal **care**, **protection** or social support **services** to children or adults in need or at risk, or adults with needs arising from illness, disability, old age or poverty.

An important role of the social care services is to provide advice and support to people in our community who are **vulnerable**. Vulnerable people might include those in need of special care, support, or protection because of age, disability, or risk of abuse or neglect. Social care services work hard to improve people's **quality of life** and wellbeing, and help care for people in lots of different situations. Some of these situations might mean providing help and advice for short periods of time whilst others may need help and support for many months or even years.

People who work in the area of social care services have a wide range of jobs and responsibilities. One very important role is that of **social worker**, someone who goes into homes and schools to help people who need support.

Sometimes families find parts of everyday life difficult to cope with. For example, this could be caused by something like a **health problem**, which social workers can help the family to deal with. In many cases, social workers will work closely with GPs, nurses, and even the police to make sure that the **whole family** is getting the care and support that they need.

Social workers also help families with the **fostering and adoption process**, and will arrange for children to be cared for if their own parents or families are unable to look after them.

Some social care workers have a lot of experience caring for older people, who might find some **everyday activities** a little more difficult than they used to. Often, only a little bit of help is needed. A social worker might pay a weekly visit to an elderly person's house, to have a chat, help them cook a meal, or make sure they are taking their medicine correctly.

What we mean when we say...

Social Worker: a person trained to help individuals, families and communities to improve their quality of life by providing a range of services and support.

Fostering and Adoption: adoption and long-term fostering are both situations which can provide a permanent home for a child. Adoption is a process which legally removes the rights and responsibilities of the child's birth parent(s), and transfers them to adoptive parent(s). A foster parent cares for a child as a parent, but does not take on the legal responsibilities of a birth parent.

Debate and evaluate:

In a group, discuss:

1 In what ways do you think social workers might be able to provide help or support to the following groups?
    - Elderly people
    - New parents
    - People with disabilities

2 Being a social worker is a very demanding job. What do you think are the most difficult aspects of being a social worker?

Read, research and decide:

1 People need different kinds of help and support during their lives. Write an account explaining some of the ways in which a social worker can help support an individual or a family.

2 What skills do you think you need to be a social worker?

CHAPTER 9: KEEPING BRITAIN SAFE – THE ARMED FORCES

The British Armed Forces look after the defence of our country. This might mean their being sent by our Government to fight in a war.

What are the Armed Forces?

There are three main parts to the Armed Forces:
* The *British Army*, which protects Britain on land.
* The *Royal Navy*, which protects Britain at sea.
* The *Royal Air Force* (often shortened to RAF), which protects Britain from the sky.

The main job of the Armed Forces is to keep Britain safe, and help enable people to live peaceful lives. Sometimes the Armed Forces are called upon to help people in times of emergency. When rivers burst their banks, you might have seen images on television of RAF helicopters rescuing people, or the army helping with flood defences.

Britain is also protected by its Intelligence Services, such as MI5 and MI6 – the shady world of spies and 007…

At the very top of the military's chain of command is our **Monarch**. Every member of the Armed Forces swears an oath of allegiance to the Monarch. The Monarch, however, doesn't actually make any real decisions about how Britain uses its Armed Forces. Instead, this is the job of our **elected politicians**, headed by the Prime Minister. Only if the Government feels it is absolutely necessary will it ask the Armed Forces to fight in a war.

The Armed Forces are here to ensure **peace**, not war. But when the Government feels it is absolutely necessary, it will ask the Armed Forces to go on operations, and sometimes, fight in a war.

Ultimately, our Government will only ask the Armed Forces to fight in a war for a 'just cause'. 'Just cause' means that there must be a moral reason for resorting to war. If a country feels that military force is necessary it must demonstrate that it has 'just cause' to do so. There are a number of different circumstances that might demonstrate 'just cause'. One of the most important reasons for a 'just war' is self-defence. Other reasons for a 'just war' might include assisting an ally who might have been invaded, or going to war to defend human rights violations.

But there is a great deal more to our Armed Forces than just fighting in wars.

The British Armed Forces can often be found helping to rebuild areas around the world that have been damaged by wars or natural disasters. This could be providing food and shelter to victims, or training local soldiers to look after themselves. Building friendships abroad helps to keep Britain safe by making sure we always have *allies* to support us. Generally, the more nations agree to work together, the stronger and safer they become.

What we mean when we say...

The Armed Forces: Britain's military services – the British Army, the Royal Navy and the Royal Air Force.

Oath of Allegiance: a promise to be loyal.

Allies: nations that are associated with others for some common cause or purpose.

Debate and evaluate:

In a group, discuss:

1 Do you think it is ever acceptable for a country to go to war? What reasons do you think would justify a 'just war'?

2 Funding the public sector is very expensive. Do you think the British Government should spend more on Britain's Armed Forces or more on the National Health Service and education? Give reasons to support your views.

Read, research and decide:

1 Explain in your own words why the British Government provides us with the Armed Forces.

2 Imagine you are Prime Minister. Write a speech that you would give in the House of Commons explaining what a 'just war' means to you, and the circumstances in which you would consider declaring war on another country.

CHAPTER 10: THE PRIME MINISTER AND THE CABINET

The brain of the public sector is the *Cabinet*. The Cabinet is a small group of around 22 Ministers who are chosen by the *Prime Minister*. Each of the Ministers in the Cabinet is called a *Cabinet Minister*. Most of the Cabinet Ministers are in charge of a part of the public sector. Each part of the public sector is called a *Department*. For example, the Minister for Health is in charge of the Department of Health, which runs the NHS. The Minister for Education is in charge of the Department of Education, which runs our schools.

Each Cabinet Minister is responsible for their own department, and decides how it should be run. Each department also has lots of *civil servants*, who help to put the ideas of the Cabinet Minister into action. The members of the Cabinet generally meet about once a week at Number 10 Downing Street, to discuss a wide range of issues facing the Government.

All of the Cabinet Ministers are very important – but there are a few you might see crop up in the newspapers more often than the others.

After the Prime Minister, the three most senior members of the Cabinet are the Chancellor of the Exchequer, the Foreign Secretary and the Home Secretary. These four positions are known as the Great Offices of State.

The *Chancellor of the Exchequer* is the Chief Finance Minister of the United Kingdom, who prepares the nation's annual budgets.

The *Foreign Secretary* deals with Britain's foreign policy and Britain's relationships with countries around the world. The Foreign Secretary is in charge of the Government department called the Foreign Office.

The *Home Secretary* has overall *responsibility* for crime policy, counter-terrorism, immigration and passports. He or she is in charge of the Government department called the Home Office.

Cabinet Ministers will work hard to help ensure that their own Government department works efficiently. As well as having an individual responsibility to look after the workings of their own department, Ministers also have a collective Cabinet responsibility. This means that individual Cabinet members must agree to accept the decisions of the whole Cabinet, and defend these decisions publicly even if as an individual they might not agree with them.

CABINET MEETING

What we mean when we say...

Cabinet: a committee of Government Ministers responsible for controlling how each Government department is run.

Prime Minister: the leader of the Government, who lives at No 10 Downing Street.

Cabinet Minister: head of a Government department.

Cabinet Collective Responsibility: (also known as Collective Ministerial Responsibility) when members of the Cabinet must publicly support all governmental decisions made in the Cabinet, even if they do not privately agree with them.

Civil Servant: someone who helps the Cabinet Minister run a Government department.

Home Secretary: the Government Minister in charge of the Home Office.

Foreign Secretary: the Government Minister in charge of the Foreign Office.

The Chancellor of the Exchequer: the Chancellor of the Exchequer is the Government's chief financial Minister. He or she has overall responsibility for the work of the Treasury.

Debate and evaluate:

In a group, discuss:

1   The Prime Minister is in charge of the Cabinet. What qualities do you think you need to have to be a good Prime Minister?

2   Discuss the roles and responsibilities of the Chancellor of the Exchequer, the Foreign Secretary and the Home Secretary. Who do you think has the most difficult job? Give reasons and examples to support your ideas.

Read, research and decide:

1   Carry out your own research on a Government department. Explain the function of the Government department. What challenges does it face? Imagine that you are the Government Minister leading this department. What ideas would you like to put into action?

2   Explain in your own words why Cabinet Ministers are required to have 'collective responsibility' for decisions made in the Cabinet. What do you think are the advantages of 'collective responsibility'?

CHAPTER 11: MANAGING BRITAIN'S MONEY – THE BUDGET

Britain's Chancellor of the Exchequer is the Government Minister responsible for running our country's budget. The Chancellor of the Exchequer has to make sure that there is enough money to pay for all of the services provided by the public sector.

The Chancellor's main job is to make sure that each department of the public sector has enough money to do its job properly, so that Britain as a whole is kept organised, provided for, cared for, and safe. The Chancellor's decisions about how to spend Britain's budget are announced in the House of Commons. They are also discussed in Cabinet meetings, so that each Cabinet Minister knows how much money their department has to spend.

The Chancellor has a very difficult job to do because each part of the public sector is very expensive and would love to have more money. But if, for example, all of the country's money went on the NHS, or on education, there would not be enough money for other parts of the public sector.

The Government receives most of its money from the tax paid by the people. If the Government decides it would like to spend more on different parts of the public sector this will usually mean that the people have to pay more money in taxes.

What we mean when we say...

Budget: a plan of how much money the country has to spend.

Tax: money paid to the Government by the citizens, like income tax paid out of the money they earn.

Debate and evaluate:

In a group, discuss:

1 Imagine you are Chancellor of the Exchequer. Consider how you would spend Britain's money. Who do you think should receive the greatest – and the smallest – share?
   - Police
   - National Health Service
   - Social Care Services
   - Education (schools and teachers)
   - Armed Forces
   - Infrastructure (which includes roads)

2 Do you think that Britons should pay more money in tax to help improve public sector services? Give reasons and examples to support your ideas.

Read, research and decide:

1 Carry out your own research on a Government department, for example, the Department of Health. Imagine that you are the Cabinet Minister in charge of this Department. Write a letter to the Chancellor of the Exchequer explaining why your department needs more money for the coming year.

2 Now imagine you are the Chancellor of the Exchequer. Every Government department has asked you for more money, but you do not have enough to meet their needs. Do you think you should ask Government departments to spend less or should you raise taxes? Give reasons and examples to support your ideas.

DO YOU REMEMBER?

Let's finish by reminding ourselves of some of the most important points we've learned:

- It is very important to be a critical thinker; this means being prepared to keep an open mind, take time to analyse and check the facts of a situation, consider more than one point of view and only then decide what you think.

- The public sector provides a range of very important services for our country.

- 999 is the number you dial if you need help in an emergency. When you dial this number, you can ask for the help of:
  - Police
  - Ambulance Service
  - Fire Brigade
  - Coastguard

- Some parts of the public sector are not always easy to see or appreciate, for example, refuse collectors.

- The public sector helps create and provide Britain's infrastructure. This includes creating and maintaining our country's roads and motorways.

- The public sector provides education for every child until at least the age of 16, by making sure that there are schools and teachers.

- One of the largest parts of the public sector is the National Health Service. The NHS provides you and your family with health care through providing you with a GP, hospitals, specialists, nurses and all of the people who work in a hospital.

- Social care workers provide short or longer term care for vulnerable members of society.

- The British Armed Forces help protect us. The Armed Forces are made up of the British Army, the Royal Navy and the Royal Air Force.

- Each part of the public sector is run by a Government Minister chosen by the Prime Minister.

- Ministers work together in the Cabinet. The Cabinet is a committee of Government Ministers led by the Prime Minister.

- The four great offices of state are The Prime Minister, the Chancellor of the Exchequer, the Foreign Secretary and the Home Secretary.

- Collective responsibility means accepting and publicly defending the group's decision even if you personally might not agree with it.

- The Chancellor of the Exchequer is the Government Minister in charge of the Government's money. He or she will determine how much money each Government department is allowed to spend and how much tax citizens should pay.